WARRIOR SCIENCE

SAMURAI
Science

Armour, Weapons and Battlefield Strategy

by Marcia Amidon Lusted

raintree

a Capstone company — publishers for children

Raintree is an imprint of Capstone Global Library Limited, a company incorporated in England and Wales having its registered office at 264 Banbury Road, Oxford, OX2 7DY – Registered company number: 6695582

www.raintree.co.uk
myorders@raintree.co.uk

Edited by Aaron Sautter
Designed by Steve Mead
Picture research by Pam Mitsakos
Production by Steve Walker
Originated by Capstone Global Library Limited
Printed and bound in China

Capstone Press would like to thank Michael Wert, PhD, of Marquette University, Wisconsin for his assistance in creating this book.

ISBN 978 1 474 71123 4
20 19 18 17 16
10 9 8 7 6 5 4 3 2 1

British Library Cataloguing in Publication Data
A full catalogue record for this book is available from the British Library.

Acknowledgements
Bridgeman Images: Look and Learn, 13, 21, 28-29; Corbis: Asian Art & Archaeology, Inc, 27; Getty Images: Culture Club, 23, Werner Forman/Universal Images Group, 24; iStockphoto: drbgaijin, 7 inset, Imre Cikajlo, 9; Library of Congress, 25; Newscom: akgphotos, 5; Shutterstock: Adam Majchrzak, 14, Barnaby Chambers, cover top background, 9 background, 20 bottom background, Eky Studio, cover, design element throughout book, elm, cover right, Elnur, cover top middle, ESOlex, back cover, honobono, 26, Milos Kontic, cover bottom, PICKY jung, cover bottom middle, psamtik, 7, 8, Romasan, 15, rudall30, 19, Volodymyr Krasyuk, cover left; Thinkstock: akiyoko, 11, Dorling Kindersley, 17

CONTENTS

THE BATTLE OF KURIKARA

The air rumbled as hundreds of samurai warriors thundered across the battlefield on horseback. The year was AD 1183. Two Japanese clans, the Minamoto and the Taira, were about to clash in a huge battle.

The Minamoto divided their army. One part waited on the battlefield. The second part **ambushed** the Taira as they moved through a mountain pass. They first distracted the Taira soldiers with whistling arrows. Then they sent a herd of oxen into the Taira army. Flaming torches were tied to the animals' horns to confuse the Taira soldiers even more. The Minamoto army's battle **tactics** killed many Taira warriors. The survivors soon fled and the Minamoto clan was victorious.

The samurai were not just soldiers. The word *samurai* means "those who serve". They were an upper class of Japanese warriors who served their *daimyos*, or lords.

ambush surprise attack

tactic plan for fighting a battle

Samurai were highly trained and effective warriors. But they owed much of their deadly abilities to science. From their armour and weapons to the way they fought, samurai relied on science to succeed. The technology of their time helped them achieve many victories over their enemies.

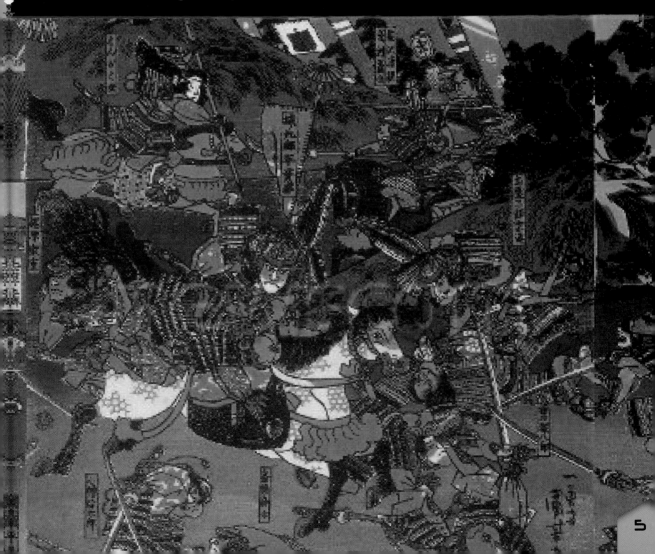

The Battle of Kurikara was fought during the Genpei War (1180–1185). During this war the Minamoto and Taira clans fought many battles for the control of Japan.

CHAPTER ONE

A SECOND SKIN

Warriors depended on body armour as a second skin to protect them from injury. Samurai warriors faced many deadly weapons during combat. To protect themselves, they used the strengths of leather and metal for maximum protection in battle.

A protective shell

Most samurai warriors did not wear plate armour made of solid metal. This type of armour was heavy and hard to move in. From about AD 80 to 1200, most samurai instead wore lamellar armour. Small rectangles of metal were sewn together and attached to leather or cloth backing. The lightweight, flexible armour provided a protective shell while allowing samurai warriors to move nimbly during a fight.

Lamellar armour was strong enough to **deflect** slicing sword cuts or arrows shot from a distance. However, it couldn't stop a direct thrust from a stabbing knife or sword. The point of a sharp weapon could slip between the metal plates to pierce a samurai's body. Lamellar armour also didn't offer much protection from the force of a heavy sword blow.

lamellar armour

Lamellar armour resembled a snake's skin made up of tiny scales. It provided protection and flexibility to a warrior during combat.

deflect to cause something to go in a different direction

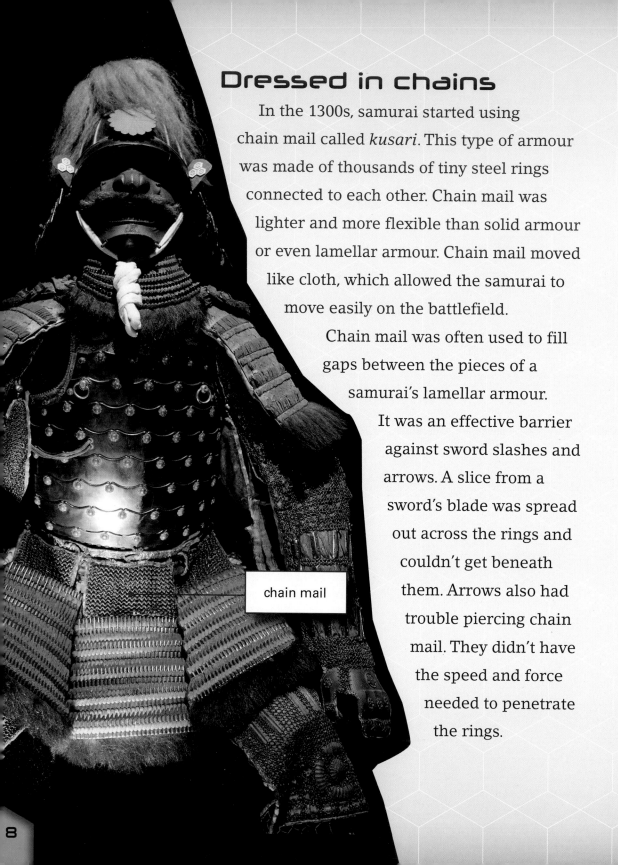

Dressed in chains

In the 1300s, samurai started using chain mail called *kusari*. This type of armour was made of thousands of tiny steel rings connected to each other. Chain mail was lighter and more flexible than solid armour or even lamellar armour. Chain mail moved like cloth, which allowed the samurai to move easily on the battlefield.

Chain mail was often used to fill gaps between the pieces of a samurai's lamellar armour. It was an effective barrier against sword slashes and arrows. A slice from a sword's blade was spread out across the rings and couldn't get beneath them. Arrows also had trouble piercing chain mail. They didn't have the speed and force needed to penetrate the rings.

chain mail

However, chain mail wasn't as effective against knives. The sharp tip of a knife, combined with the force of an enemy's thrusting arm, could pierce the small rings. Chain mail was also ineffective against heavy blows. The flexible rings were not strong enough to **disperse** the energy of the blow.

THE AGE OF BULLETS

In the 1500s, samurai began using guns in battle. To protect themselves from bullets, they developed new armour made from iron plates. Solid iron was strong enough to withstand the force of a bullet. The new plate armour was curved to fit a warrior's body. This shape made it harder for bullets to strike. They were often deflected by the armour's curved surface. Plate armour provided great protection. But it was heavy and limiting. Samurai warriors couldn't move easily in the solid armour and quickly grew tired while wearing it.

disperse to spread out over a wide area

Strong head protection

One of the most important pieces of a samurai's armour was his helmet. Called a *kabuto*, the helmet's dome section was made of rounded metal plates fastened together with rivets. Flexible lamellar armour flaps were then attached to the base of the helmet. These flaps helped protect a samurai's neck from sword swipes during combat.

A kabuto's round shape helped deflect blows during a fight. Swords and arrows were more likely to glance off the helmet's curves. The rounded metal also spread the energy of a direct blow over a larger area. This kept the energy from being absorbed by a warrior's head, which could cause serious damage.

Samurai sometimes added decorations to their helmets. Some warriors added **crests** or animal horns. Others wore fierce steel masks with exaggerated features. These masks were usually in the form of demons or evil spirits. They were meant to frighten enemies while protecting the samurai's face and neck.

FACT Samurai often wore billowing cloth cloaks called *horos* on their backs for extra protection in battle. As a warrior rode his horse, the wind inflated the cloak like a balloon. Enemy arrows bounced off the cloak to protect the samurai and his horse.

The riveted plates of a kabuto's round dome made it thicker and stronger than a single layer of metal.

rounded metal plates

lamellar flaps

crest ornament worn to symbolize one's family or clan

CHAPTER TWO

LEGENDARY WEAPONS

To be effective warriors, samurai used several types of deadly weapons. Whether they used swords, bows and arrows, or specialized blades, a samurai's weapons provided certain advantages in combat.

Samurai swords

Samurai warriors were most famous for their deadly *tachi* and *katana* swords. Experts believe that medieval Japanese swordsmiths made some of the best weapons in the world. They used a special process to make their swords especially strong and sharp.

FACT Today, high quality samurai swords are still made by hand using traditional methods. Skilled craftsmen still use the same process used in ancient times.

Samurai swords were some of the highest quality weapons ever made. They were sharp enough to pierce enemy armour and strong enough to resist breaking during combat.

First, both hard and soft steel were created with iron ore and charcoal. Hard steel contained a high amount of carbon. Soft soft steel contained less carbon. A swordsmith covered a core of soft steel with a layer of hard steel. The layers of steel were then repeatedly heated, folded and hammered until several layers were bonded together. This process resulted in a blade that was extremely hard, strong and sharp. Because of the strength of the metal, the blade's edge stayed razor-sharp.

Fighting on a curve

Most samurai swords had a curved shape. This shape maximized the impact force by focusing it in a smaller area. This design, combined with the swords' light weight, made them especially effective in combat. However, samurai occasionally used straight swords for thrusting attacks. A straight sword's sharp point could be lined up with its hilt and the warrior's grip. This allowed him to make powerful thrusting strikes.

Pole arms

Some samurai fought with a *naginata*, which was a sharp blade attached to a long wooden pole. The blade could be 25 to 61 centimetres (10 to 24 inches) long. The naginata was effective when it was swung in wide circles. It could cut through a horse's legs or a warrior on foot. The pole's length gave a warrior an advantage by allowing him to attack an enemy from a safer distance.

 A *katana*'s design helped samurai make swift slashing attacks to slice through an enemy's armour.

The lower end of a naginata was often tipped with an *ishizuki*. This sharp metal cap could be thrust between plates of an anemy's armour.

ishizuki

Bows and arrows

Many samurai were expert archers. They were famous for shooting accurately, even while riding full speed on a horse. Samurai bows were constructed from strips of mulberry wood and bamboo. The bows were lightweight, strong and flexible.

The **physics** of archery require an even pull on the bowstring to shoot accurately. And to shoot from horseback required great skill. A samurai had to hold his bow high while notching an arrow to avoid bumping his horse. He also had to shoot to the side of the horse to avoid spooking it as he rode. Samurai practised for many hours to correctly position their horses and shoot accurately while riding.

Samurai used arrows made of bamboo with duck feathers for **fletching**. Arrowheads were made of iron and had different shapes for different uses. Scissorlike arrowheads were used for cutting cords on armour. Sharp points were effective for injuring or killing the enemy. One special type of arrow had a pierced bulb of wood or deer horn shaped like a turnip. Air passed through the holes in the bulb to make a whistling sound. These whistling arrows, called *kabura-ya*, were used to frighten enemies and signal the beginning of a battle.

physics science that studies matter, energy, force and motion

fletching feathers of an arrow

A samurai had to be careful when shooting a bow while riding a horse. He didn't want to risk hitting or spooking his own horse with the arrows while riding into combat.

CHAPTER THREE

TRAINING TO FIGHT

A samurai's weapons and armour were very important. But they were only tools. To be effective in battle, a samurai had to know how to use them. Above all, he needed to be well trained.

Martial arts training

Physical training was very important to be a skilled warrior. Samurai trained in martial arts to improve their balance, flexibility and **coordination**. This training also improved a samurai's overall strength, speed and endurance.

In battle, samurai needed to move and fight without thinking about it. To achieve this, they trained repeatedly using the same body motions. This training helped create "muscle memory". When muscles are used in the same way over and over again, a person can eventually perform those actions without conscious effort. This type of training allowed a samurai to fight using his **instincts**. It also helped reduce the risk of mistakes that could lead to injury or death.

Samurai warriors also practised defensive moves such as throwing opponents, joint locks and blocking. A skilled warrior could still fight effectively even if he found himself without any weapons.

Samurai practised constantly to keep their fighting skills sharp. They knew that the best warriors fought using only their instincts during battle.

coordination ability to control body movements

instinct knowing something naturally without being told about it

Horseback training

Samurai were highly skilled warriors on horseback. To fight or shoot well while on a horse required strong legs and great balance. To achieve this, samurai constantly practised their fighting skills while riding horses. Over time, their legs grew strong. They also learned to keep their bodies balanced correctly to ride and fight at the same time.

Samurai learned how to control their horses in battle using only their legs and feet. When shooting a bow, a rider had to drop the reins. He controlled his horse using only foot and leg movements, or by shifting his weight in the saddle. Controlling a horse this way allowed the archer greater focus to aim and hit a moving target.

ADVANTAGES OF HORSEBACK FIGHTING

Fighting on horseback gave samurai a great advantage in battle. Horses allowed the warriors to move around quickly on the battlefield. The horse's speed also added to the force of sword strikes against enemy fighters. Arrows could be shot more accurately over longer distances from horseback than from the ground. Shooting an arrow from a horse allowed the arc of the arrow's flight to start higher. This meant it could travel farther to hit a distant enemy target.

Samurai archers practised controlling horses with their legs and feet for many hours. This skill allowed them to use their hands during battle while directing their horses on the battlefield.

CHAPTER FOUR

BATTLEFIELD TACTICS

Science gave samurai an advantage in their equipment and training. But they also had to understand the **terrain** they fought on. Whether fighting in an open field or in a mountain pass, science played a role in samurai battlefield strategies.

Battlefield terrain

Samurai battle techniques often depended on the kinds of terrain where battles took place. Flat, open areas were good for horseback fighting. There were few trees with low hanging branches to brush riders off their horses or entangle them. These flat areas also had few hills or places with uncertain footing.

However, rocky ground and steep hills were more difficult for horses. Rough ground could damage a horse's hooves or injure its legs. Long climbs up steep hills could tire horses quickly and make them less effective in battle. Fighting on steep slopes could also result in a horse stumbling or losing its balance during a fight.

For these reasons, fighting on foot was better for battles in mountains, heavy forests or rocky areas. With only two feet to manage, foot soldiers were more nimble than horses. They could keep their footing better and scramble more easily over rocks or around trees.

The land often determined what kind of tactics samurai used in battle. Uneven or slippery ground usually required samurai to face enemies on foot instead of on horses.

terrain surface of the land

Battle formations

Samurai used many formations to achieve success on the battlefield. Formations were used both for attacking the enemy and protecting the army's own soldiers.

One common battle formation was the *Hoshi*, or arrowhead, formation. Foot soldiers with guns called arquebuses first weakened the enemy's front line. Then a wedge of samurai on horseback could punch through to deal major damage to the enemy's forces. Other battle formations included the *Kakuyoku* (crane's wing), *Gyorin* (fish scales) and *Choda* (long snake). Each of these could be modified and used as necessary based on the type of terrain the samurai were fighting on.

During the Siege of Osaka Castle (1615), Tokugawa forces used several successful battle formations to defeat the Toyotomi clan.

FACT

In the heat of battle, it could be hard to tell which soldiers belonged to which army. Samurai wore small flags called *sashimono* to identify the army to which they belonged.

Shield walls

Samurai on horseback could easily move and retreat from the enemy. But foot soldiers had to find ways to protect themselves during combat. One method they used was to link their shields together to create a wall called a *kaidate*. Linking shields provided much greater protection than each soldier holding his own. The linked shield wall was very strong and each warrior was partly protected by his neighbour's shield. Tree branches and bushes were also used to create barriers, called *sakamogi*, against horsemen. But these barriers were not as quick and easy to set up. They were also not as strong as a solid shield wall.

Battlefield medicine

As in any battle, samurai warriors suffered injuries. Battle wounds were often treated with *yomogi*, or mugwort. Sometimes dried horse **manure** was used for treating wounds. The manure was packed into the wound. Then the wound was sewn shut with mulberry root fibres and sprinkled with pollen from cattails.

Injured samurai might also be given a mixture of water and horse manure or **urine** to drink. It was thought that manure contained nutrients that could help with healing. And animal urine was thought to reduce the chances of infection.

Warriors often also took ritual baths after a battle. They may not have realized it, but these baths helped clean and purify battle wounds to prevent infection and help them heal.

← Samurai used the mugwort plant on wounded warriors to help stop the bleeding.

manure animal waste

urine liquid waste that people and animals pass out of their bodies

Medicine wasn't very advanced during the time of the samurai. Several crude treatments were used to try to heal wounded warriors. Some samurai recovered, but seriously injured warriors often died.

Samurai scientists

The samurai lived and fought before many scientific principles were known. However, science played a large role in their equipment and combat methods.

Samurai weapons and armour used science to give the warriors an edge in combat. Specialized steel and forging techniques made their weapons especially deadly. Their armour was designed to give them flexibility and speed while it protected them in combat. Samurai trained for many hours every day to strengthen their bodies and sharpen their fighting skills. They also knew how to use the natural terrain to their advantage. With the help of science, the samurai became some of history's most famous warriors.

FACT

Samurai warriors began their training at 5 years old. Their fathers, older brothers or uncles usually taught them. In addition to weapons and martial arts skills, they also learned the basic customs and traditions of being a samurai.

ambush surprise attack

coordination ability to control body movements

crest ornament worn to symbolize one's family or clan

deflect to cause something to go in a different direction

disperse to spread out over a wide area

fletching feathers of an arrow

instinct knowing something naturally without being told about it

manure animal waste

physics science that studies matter, energy, force and motion

tactic plan for fighting a battle

terrain surface of the land

urine liquid waste that people and animals pass out of their bodies

Comprehension questions

1. Why were samurai swords considered better quality than most other swords? What features did they have that made them special?

2. In what ways were lamellar armour and chain mail different from plate armour? If you were a samurai warrior, which type of armour would you choose for combat?

Books

A Samurai Castle (Spectacular Visual Guides), Fiona MacDonald (Scribo, 2017)

Ninjas and Samurai: A Nonfiction Companion to Magic Tree House #5: Night of the Ninjas (Magic Tree House Fact Tracker) Mary Pope Osborne and Natalie Pope Boyce (Random House, 2014)

Samurai (Fearless Warriors), Rupert Matthews (Franklin Watts, 2016)

Websites

www.encyclopedia.com/topic/samurai.aspx#1
Several articles on samurai, including one about samurai clothing and fashion.

samuraikids.com.au/samuraifacts.html
Download fact sheets to find out about legendary samurai.

www.youngsamurai.com/site/YOUN/Templates/General. aspx?pageid=5&cc=GB
Learn more about weapons, the art of zen and the difference between samurai and ninja.